SELECTED POEMS
1957–2009

Mikhail Yeryomin

SELECTED POEMS

1957–2009

translated by J. Kates

White Pine Press / Buffalo, New York

White Pine Press
P.O. Box 236
Buffalo, New York 142 01
www.whitepine.org

Publication of this book was made possible, in part, by grants
from the Cliff Becker Endowment for the Literary Arts, the
Creative Writing Program at the University of Missouri; and
with public funds from the New York State Council on the Arts,
a State Agency.

State of the Arts

NYSCA

Some of the translations in this collection have been previously published in *The Fjords
Review*, *Hawai'i Review*, *Parthenon West*, *Pusteblume*, *Stand* (United Kingdom), *Two
Lines*, *World Literature Today*, and in the anthology *In the Grip of Strange Thoughts*
(Zephyr: 1999).

Cover image: by Karuna Licht
First Edition.
ISBN: 978-1-935210-61-0
Printed and bound in the United States of America.
Library of Congress Number: 2014930816

INTRODUCTION

For more than half a century, Mikhail Yeryomin[1] has been writing poetry unique in Russian literature. Each of more than two hundred fifty poems (so far) is a discrete eight-line stanza. When he publishes them, each one takes up a separate page. Some are accompanied by notes. Over the years, these form a sweep of verse that has its only English analogue, perhaps, in Berryman's *Dream Songs* or Pound's *Cantos*, and none at all in Russian poetry. (In a French tradition, Maurice Scève's Renaissance sequence *Délie: Objet de plus haute vertu* may come closest to Yeryomin's achievement, but the virtuous love-object of the Russian poet's obsession is the whole living world over a stretch of time from Creation until now.)

Mikhail Fyodorovich Yeryomin was born in 1936 in the northern Caucasus but grew up in Leningrad, where he studied in the Philology Department of the Leningrad State University and graduated from the Herzen Institute. A like-minded, good friend of Joseph Brodsky before that poet's exile, Yeryomin is a playwright and a translator (of T. S. Eliot, Hart Crane, W. B. Yeats, M. Ikbal, Khushkhal-khan Khattak, among others) who saw few of his poems published in his homeland during the Soviet period. Instead, his work appeared in émigré journals like *Kontinent* and *Ekho*. The first

---

[1] In an academic transliteration of the poet's name, it is written *Eremin*. The poet himself prefers a transliteration that more closely approximates the English pronunciation. Because he has been published in German translation also (*V.* the anthology *Moderne russische Poesie seit 1966*, ed. Walter Thümler, Oberbaum Verlag, Berlin: 1990) his surname sometimes appears as *Jerjomin*.

volume of his poems (in Russian) was published in the United States in 1986, and then in 1991 in Moscow. Each book is a cumulative edition to and a selection from his previous work, and each carries the same title: *Stikhotvorenia* (Poems). So far, there have been seven of these (1986, 1991, 1996, 1998, 2002, 2005, 2009). Yeryomin was awarded the Andrey Bely Prize in 1999.

The best description of Yeryomin's poetry comes from Mikhail Aizenberg's comprehensive essay "A Few Others"[2]:

> "Generally speaking, there is no school you could put Eremin [Yeryomin] in, even conditionally. . . . The assigned eight-line canon, the absence (except for his early verse) of rhyme—all this is no accident. In general, Eremin's texts can contain nothing accidental. the verse's superdense fabric would offer terrible resistance to anything too free or casual. . . . [T]he verbal transformations obey their own laws, and the poems grow like crystals. . . . They strive to take in everything, to become everything. . . . This kind of poetics, woven together with maximally intense thought, has no direct analogues or traces of obvious influences."

Nevertheless, Yeryomin has been associated with the Leningrad "Philological School" of the 1960s and 70s embracing primarily Vladimir Uflyand, Leonid Vinogradov, Sergey Kulle, Mikhail Krasilnikov, Yuri Mikhailov, Aleksandr Kondratov and Lev Loseff as well as Yeryomin (the only one of the group still alive) which was experimenting with the possibilities of *vers libre* when that kind of thing was generally treated warily in Russian poetry, and which flourished as a community until the emigration of Loseff in the mid 1970s. Yeryomin's work stands out even from the work of his close contemporaries and associates by the abundant variety embedded in his steadfast regularity of form.

The late Genrikh Sapgir wrote of Yeryomin,[3] "When I read these eight-line poems it seems to me from time to time that I am

---

[2] translated by Marian Schwartz in Russian Studies in Literature, spring 1996, pp 28–9
[3] *http://www.rvb.ru/np/publication/sapgir4.htm#49*, my own translation

watching from inside a green blade of grass, infinitely magnified. Latin and Greek words and Egyptian hieroglyphics are laid out on the page in a universal inscription, a portrait of nature itself." Using the languages of science, music, hieroglyphics (real and invented) and other esoterica to construct the octaves, he is very particular about his rhythms and his sounds.

Because Yeryomin has a fair command of English, I work more closely with him than with most of the other poets I translate. As a translator, I am more opportunistic than theoretical. My aim has been to convey in English, by whatever means necessary, the content and force of the original, and I am flexible in my approach—sometimes adhering closely to original formal constructs, sometimes deviating from them. Yeryomin's work demands the eight-line format, sensitivity to technical terms, rhythms and wordplay. Rhythms, of course, are linguistic constructs—and for these as well as for specific vocabulary, I have needed to consult most closely with the poet, who has sometimes made demands that have had to be negotiated. In at least one case, he invited me to translate what lies behind the words, rather than what the words indicate. In another case, he asked for a rhythmic impossibility in English. Equivalence therefore sometimes replaces congruence. But my primary acknowledgment must be to him, for his encouragement as well as his contention, both of which sharpened the focus of this work. I am grateful also for the perspective of others' translations of a few of Yeryomin's poems, and especially for one word lifted (with permission) from Michael Molnar.

Боковитые зёрна премудрости,
Изначальную форму пространства,
Всероссийскую святость и смутность
И болот журавлиную пряность
Отыскивать в осенней рукописи,
Где следы оставила слякоть,
Где листы, словно платья луковицы,
Слезы прячут в складках.

1957

Polyhedral kernels of wisdom,
Primordial form of space.
All-Russian holiness, hodgepodge
And the herony tang of swampland
To be searched out in autumnal writing,
Where the slush has left its traces,
Where leaves, like the skirts of an onion
Conceal tears in their creases.

1957

Сшивает портниха на швейной машинке,
Подобно дождю, голубое с зеленым,
Дождю, который окном изломан,
Как лодкою камышинки.
Гром за окном покашливает.
Капли дождя к стеклу прилипают,
Полузеленая каждая
И полуголубая.

1957

The seamstress stitches on a sewing machine,
Light blue with deep green, like rain,
Rain broken by the window
As reeds are broken by a little boat.
A thunderstorm coughs outside the window.
Raindrops cling to the glass,
Every single one of them half green
And half light blue.

1957

Л. Лифшицу

Переплавил не в золото — в никель
Рыжий алхимик снега.
На небе, как в Голубиной книге,
Еврейская грамота березняка.
Равнины черны, как раввины,
Заполнены реки щепой от весла,
В совиных глазнцах овинов,
Как мышь, зашуршала весна.

1957

for L. Lifshitz (A. Loseff)

The auburn alchemist of snow
Transmuted not into gold but nickel.
In the heavens, as in the Book of Doves,
A Hebrew primer of birches.
Ravines as black as rabbis,
Rivers running with shards of oars,
In owlish eye-sockets of granaries,
Spring, like a mouse, was rustling.

1957

Пальба из-под ног уходила, как палуба,
Падал пушкарь на осеннюю подстилку,
Словно батальонный баловень
Бил о поле затылком.
Павшего запеленает в кисет,
Формалином и соком древесным пропахший,
Маркитант-носитель косы
памяти императора Павла.

1958

A cannonade careered underfoot like an anchor-deck,
The gunner downed on the autumn detritus,
As the pet of a battalion
Bumped the back of his head on the boards.
The pig-tailed sutler swaddles the fallen one
in a tobacco-pouch,
permeated with formaline and sap,
a pavilion commemorating the Emperor Paul.

1958

Там тени павших пашут ресницах,
Там, в царстве доадмовой смекалки,
Кентавры негодуют по-оленьи,
В соперников втыкая томагавки.

1958

Там, кумачом завесив небо комнат,
Перистый вепрь выпрыгивает в дым;
Нагие ноги ноют в катакомбах,
Перебираемые, как лады.

1958

There shadows plough fallen eyelashes,
There, in the realm of pre-adamic intelligence,
Centaurs take umbrage like deer,
Burying tomahawks into competitors.

1958

There, a sky of rooms hung with red calico,
A feathery wild boar breaks out into the smoke;
Naked legs lament in the catacombs,
Being fingered like harmonies.

1958

Строител первого в мире моста
К месту строительства бревна таскал и доски,
Ладил настил, а потом настал
Час первой повозки.
Плотник локти положил на перила,
Трубкой украсил довольное лицо,
Выплеснул на рубаху бороды белила,
И стало мостостроение ремеслом отцов.

1958

The builder of the first bridge in the world
Dragged beams and boards to the construction site,
Readied the planking—and then began
The hour of the first vehicle.
The carpenter laid his elbows on the railing,
His contented face adorned by a pipe,
The whitewash of his beard splashed on his bib,
And bridge-building became an ancestral craft.

1958

Терлось тельце телка
Об устойчивые стены стойла.
Нос коровий тельца толкал
Выводил на пустырь просторный.
Теленок вышел из коровника,
Стадности не стыдясь, пересек пустырь
И нежился в поле перстым курортником,
Жил, пережевывая стебли и лепестки.

1958

The cow cuddled the calf
All through the stalls of the stable,
The cow's nose nudged the calf
Out into the open lot.
The calf came out of the cow-barn
One of the herd, loped through the lot
And basked in the field like a dappled sunbather,
Asked for nothing but stems and petals.

1958

По-за краквой ходит селезень,
То прищелкнет клювом плоским,
То крылом взмахнет, как сеятель,
Глазом ласковым поблескивая,
Чтоб, живущий возле заводи,
Мальчуган нашел гнездо,
Чтоб яишенные завтраки
Подавала мать на стол.

1958

The drake pays court to the duck,
He snaps his flat beak,
He swings his wing like a man sowing seed,
His affectionate eye glitters now and again,
So that the good boy who lives
Near the creek can find the nest,
So his mother can serve up eggs
At the breakfast table.

1958

Сохатый крест рогов, как идола,
Возносит над кустарником.
Корову не выигрывает, а выпиливает
Из самых нежных мышц соперника.
Звучит в юдоли гонный рог
И ранит бок до соли.
Вдыхают важенки пригожие
Жестокий запах отца и сына.

1959

An elk lifts a cross of branching antlers,
like an idol, over the underbrush.
He cuts out his right to the cow
From the tenderest muscles of his rival.
The implacable antler clacks in the glen
And inflicts a wound deep in the flank,
While comely virgin doe breathe in
The cruel scent of father and son.

1959

Золотое перышко выпало из облака,
Словно колечко из наволочки.
Бабушкины сумерки в окна заболоченные
Барабанят острыми ягодами волчьими.
Над крыльцом опята эоловой цепочкой.
Ноги светлым мячиком по ступенькам спрыгивают,
Каждая туфелька подобна красной шапочке,
Лукошку с белыми подарками.

1960

A golden little plume fell out of a cloud,
Like a ringlet of down from a pillow.
Grandmother's twilight drums with pointed
Wolfish berries on the swampy windows.
Over the porch æolian mushrooms in single file.
Feet hop down the steps like a bright little ball,
Each shoelet like a little red riding hood,
A handbasket filled with white gifts.

1960

Печальный сезон многобожья,
Изломанность зонтичных над падшей травой,
Языческий плач чернобелых болот,
Из прозрачных деревьев сотворение терема,
Утренней церкви заокнное пение,
Стакан золотого заморского чая,
Свеча, обнаженная светом небесным,
И юная дева в преддверье плеча.

1961

A sorrowful season of polytheism,
Fractured umbellifrates over fallen grass,
A pagan lament of black-and-white marshland,
The creation of a tower from transparent trees,
Plainchant through the windows of morning churches,
A glass of golden tea from abroad,
A candle undressed by a heavenly light,
And a young virgin on the threshold of a shoulder.

1961

Животные обуваются в снежные следы
Или врадают в логово.
Растения гонимы холодом
В лабиринты корней и луковиц.
Люди уменьшают до размеров обуви
Присущие водоемам ладьи.
Подо льдом, как под теплым небом,
Фотолуг, Фотолес, Фотолето.

1962

Animals put on their shoes in snowy tracks
Or go to ground.
Plants tormented by the cold
Into labyrinths of roots and bulbs.
People shrink as small as shoes
Like little boats in rivers and ponds.
Under the ice, as under a warm sky,
Photomeadow, photowood, photosummer.

1962

$$k = 0$$

И дробь це больших прожекторов
Стоящих валит с ног на тень.
Подобный обескнииженной этажерке
Парит би-Планк над Т Ньютона,
Над часовыми, значительными, как пожарные,
Над живородящими тополями,
Над белковым покровом России,
Библиотекой и футбольным полем.

1963

$$k = 0$$

I slash c of large searchlights
Fells what's standing into shadow.
Like a bookcase emptied of books,
B-Planck hovers over T Newton,
Over watchmen as meaningful as firefighters,
Over viviparous poplars,
Over the albuminous cloak of Russia,
A library and a soccer field.

1963

$x^3 + y^3 = 3axy$ есть ничто.
Ствол не насос, а высохший колодец.
Изоамиламина генератор
Жует подземные лучи.
Нелетний свет слепит растения.
Кольчуга склеренхимы холодна.
Засвечены фотоладони клёнов.
Горит осины санбенито.

1966

[Их куб плюс игрек куб минус три а икс игрек . . .] — «Декартов лист»

Изоамиламин — пахучее вещество, выделяемое самкой майского
жука

$x^3 + y^3 = 3axy$ is nothingness.
A tree-trunk is not a pump, but a dry well.
A generator of isoamilamin
Munches on underground rays.
An unsummery light dazzles the plants.
Cold is the mail-shirt of sklerenchemistry.
The photopalms of maples overexposed.
The sanbenito of the aspen flames.

1966

x cube plus y cube minus three axy: the "Folium of Descartes" = jasmine leaf

isoamilamin is a strong-smelling substance given off by the female may-bug

Y ❀ ⟨⟩ ⚖ 🚁

Гелиопте́р гостиницы высотной,
Как перистое небо над подлекшим
Пришкольным сквером.
Владелицы осенних ранцев
Трепещут над сетями «классов»,
Уносит вдаль летучки кленов
Поток асфальта, огибая сквер.

1971

Y — антенна

❀ — лотос *(др.-египетск.)*

⟨⟩ — экскаватор

⚖ — справедливость *(др.-египетск.)*

🚁 — вертолет

Y ⚘ ⛏ ⚖ ⚙

Helioptér of a skyscraper hotel,
Like a feathery sky over a faded
Public park beside a school.
The owners of autumnal knapsacks
Tremble over networks of hopscotch.
A flow of asphalt circling the park
Carries the maple wings far away.

1971

Y — antenna

⚘ — lotus (ancient Egyptian)

⛏ — backhoe

⚖ — justice (ancient Egyptian)

⚙ — helicopter

Подобный медной орхидее
Кентавр о двух стволах
Воздушный корень изогнул,
Чешуйчатый и ядовитый.
Как между префиксом с суффиксом,
Змея меж πετρος и Петром. Вечнозеленый
(Не хлрофилл, а $CuCO_3$)
Вознесся лавровый привой.

1972

I behold idols carved . . .
G. R. Derzhavin

Exactly like a coppery orchid,
A centaur with two trunks
Entwined an airy root
Scaly and venomous.
As between prefix and suffix,
A snake between πετρος and Peter. Evergreen
(Not chlorophyll, but $CuCO_3$)
a graft of laurel reared up.

1972

Над сквером дом — букет вечерних окон.
Собор от мира сквером огражден.
Лист золотой намотан, словно локон,
На ту же ветвь, которой был рожден.
Осенный день, на грех и слезы падкий,
Молчанье и раскаянье поймет,
Оставив пепел от письма в лампадке
И в медальоне дьявола помет.

1972

The house over the park is a bouquet of evening windows.
A cathedral fenced off from the world by a garden.
A golden leaf is wound like a ringlet
On the very twig that gave it birth.
An autumn day, susceptible to sin and tears,
Will understand silence and repentance,
Ashes of a letter have been left in the icon-lamp
And devil's dung in the medallion.

1972

Поселок (В сумерках туман подобен
Прасубстантиву: наблюдатель — «. . . пред
Святым Его Евангелием и животворящим
Крестом . . .» — становится свидетелем аблактировки
Инфинитива и супина.) сходство
С полузатопленным челном и средним членом
Сравненья мышц стрижа с пружиною зажима,
Забытого на бельевой веревке, обретает.

1977

A settlement (In twilight a fog similar
To the protosubstantive: the observer—"before
His Holy Gospel and life-giving
Cross . . ."—becomes a witness of the ablactation
Of the infinitive and the supine.) is a simulacrum
of a kindled canoe and the middling member
of the comparison of a martin's muscles with an elastic clamp,
forgotten on a clothesline, found.

1977

Повилика, прильнувшая к стеблю,
Бледный витень, чье тело длиной с его жизнь —
Дериват ли от vita? Гаплоия
Композиты из vita и тень?
Или плеть? Аксельбант родовитого льна
Или ядопровод? Или тирса лоза? Или —
«. . . The laws impressed on matter by the Creator . . .»
Селекционерская гордость Мойр?

1977

Гаплогия — гаплология.

Ch. Darwin, M. A. *The Origin of Species*. "Recapitulation and conclusion."

A dodder clinging tightly to its stem,
Pallid viten, a body long as its life—
Does it derive from *vita*? Haplogy
Compounded from *vita* and *tenebræ*?
Or a lash? An aiguilette of aristocratic flax
Or a poison duct? Or a vine of thyrsus? Or —
"... *the laws impressed on matter by the Creator* ..."—
The selectionist pride of the three Fates?

1977

Haplogy = haplology

Ch. Darwin, M. A. *The Origin of Species*. "Recapitulation and conclusion."

Растениям и тьма, и свет желанны.
(Догадка элинна: νυχθ-ήμερον — не зло-добро, а сутки.)
В их верованьях нет ни прозорливых звезд,
Ни страха перед полночью, ни крика петуха,
Ни мрака преисподней, ни паденья ниц пред солнцем —
Им прелставляется Творец утро-вечерний цветом.
Спряжение глагола «быть» — модель
Метагенеза (и бессмертия) былинки.

1977

νυχθ-ήμερον — ночь-день

Plants wish for both darkness and light.
(The Greeks guessed: νυχθ-ήμερον is not evil-good, but the
day's round.)
Their faith includes neither sagacious stars,
Nor any fear of midnight, nor any cock-crow,
Nor gloom of the Underworld, nor groveling sun-worship—
The morning-evening Creator introduces introduces color.
The conjugation of the verb "to be" is a pattern
Of the metagenesis (and immortality) of a blade of grass.

1977

νυχθ-ήμερον = night-day

Ираиде

Сомкнула веки. Не вступать, а погружаться
В сокрытый ими сад. Деревья —
Еще не алфавит, уже не древние аллеи текста.
Любовь — еще вторая изгородь. Движенье —
Уже не ноша, но еще не ниша.

Не словом открывают губы
Лучистый взгляд жемчужин
Над моим лицом.

1978

for Iraida

She closed her eyelids. Not to step into, but be plunged
Into a garden hidden beneath them. The trees
Not yet alphabet, now no longer ancient alleys of text.
Love is still a second hedge. Movement
No longer burdensome, but even less a burrow.

Lips do not discover with a word
The radiant appearance of pearls
Over my face.

1978

Пир августа. Азычество лампасов и лампад.
Ватрушка — в каждом угольке готовый вспыхнуть
Зеленым пламенем творожный язычок —
Подсолнуха. Стручок гороха скалит зубы,
Расколотый, изогнутый древнейшей шуткой
Равновеликости на взглял с земли
Луны и соднца. Платье юной горожанки —
Поблекший крапп, полегший лен.

1979

Крапп — марена

Feast of August. Aborigin of trouser-stripes and icon-lamps.
Cheesecake—each ember ready to flare up
A little curd tongue like a green flicker—
Sunflowers. A peapod bares its teeth,
Disruptive, twisted like an ancient joke
Equivalence in looking from the earth
Moon and sun. The dress of a young townswoman—
Withering madder, flattened flax.

1979

Отпавший от высокой ветви лист
Немеет, оказавшись на обочине,
Трепещет, как чахоточная грудь,
Переворачивается четыре раза,
Хватая воздух беззащитным телом,
И, распластавшись, замирает, медленней,
Чем ликогалы выполз, превращаясь
В шепот ветхой трубки.

                                        1980

A leaf that fell from the high branch
Goes mute, having landed on the side of the road,
It trembles, like a consumptive breast,
Turns itself over and over four times,
Gulping the air by its defenseless body,
And having sprawled, grows still, more slowly,
Than the crawl of a lycogalla becoming
The whisper of a decrepit pipelet.

1980

И странствовал,
Совсем как тот, чье бытие — не чаша ли
Той трещины,
Прозрачный волосок которой
От сотворения в каолинит заложен
Единственным свидетелем того,
Что видится нам в гефсиманской тишине
Под сводом сада.

1981

And he wandered
Exactly like him whose existence—is it not a chalice
Of that crack
Whose transparent hairlet introduced
From the Creation into kaolinite
By the only witness of what
Appears to us in the quiet of Gethsemane
Under the garden arch.

1981

Возня без названия в зарослях
Брусники и призрак —
В чужом непрозрачном плаще — слизняка,
И дряблые логвища водяной мелюзги,
И алчет, в дупле притаясь, фиолетовый
Прыжок, и теряющий векторность вечер
Не волен в трелевочных ковах и бледен,
Словно Нарцисс с ссадиной от скулы до скулы.

1983

There is a nameless bustling in the thicket
Of red whortleberry and a ghost—
In the opaque, and someone else's raincoat—of a slug,
And the flaccid dens of aquatic small fry,
And the violet leap, hiding in a hollow, starves
while the evening, losing its vector,
Is entrapped in its hobbles and pale,
Like Narcissus with a scratch from cheek to cheek.

                    1983

Валькирии томятся о шахиде.
Поток шоссе вращает подливные
Колеса. Алущий ручей гюрзы
Противу перистальтики бархана
Струится. С талией песочного хронометра оса
Ныряет вглубь своей обители. Течет
Отара вверх по склону. Вещ
Лакунами протектор минарета.

1985

Valkyries languish over a shakhid.
The torrent of the highway turns an undershot
Paddlewheel. The hungering rivulet of a viper
Streams against the peristalsis
Of a sand-dune. A wasp with an hour-glass
Waist dives deep into its dwelling. A flock
Of sheep flows up the slope.
Lacunæ of the minaret's protector enclose a prophecy.

1985

На подступах к развенчанной столице
И царственна,
Как бронзовый каузатив, что оживлен
Лишь мертвой зеленью, подобной
Подтекам ив, река,
И прописные — киноварь по медной сини — вербы
На противоположном берегу
Безмолвны.

1985

On the approaches to the deposed capital,
Still regal,
Like a bronze causative, which is animated
Only by a dead green, similar
To the dripping of weeping willows, the river,
And uppercase—vermilion on copper blue—willows
On the opposite shore
Speechless.

1985

Следить бег низких облаков
И пресмыкание далекой электрички. Pópulus Vulgaris
Толпой (Избранничество — не искус ли?)
И вдоль дорог выстраивается. Прониккнуть
Ленотром или (Оттиск аватары
На глине или благодать?) Алкидом —
Одна двенадцатая дюжины побед —
В усадьбу Гесперид?

1985

Ленотр — Версальский парк, Фоненбло и т. д.

To follow the races of low clouds
And the reptilian crawl of a distant train. *Pópulus Vulgaris*
En masse (Isn't a referendum a temptation?)
And alongside, the construction of roads. To penetrate
By means of Le Nôtre or (The Impression of an avatar
In clay, or a blessing?) with Alcides—
One twelfth of a dozen victories—
In the Garden of the Hesperides?

1985

Le Nôtre — The park at Versailles, Fontainebleau, etc.

Фонарь. Отсутствие. Аптека.
И ртутна наледь на металле
Патрульного автомобиля. В тарлатановых тюниках
Метель разучивает па сколопендреллы.
А полуптица-полутяжесть
Белее крыльев, явственных во сне.
И ни задатка, и ни предостережения
Не отразили святочные зеркала.

1986

Street lamp. Something missing. Drugstore.
And an icy crust like mercury on the metal
Of a patrol car. In tarlatan tutus
The snow storm studies the dance-step of scolopendrella.
But semibird and semiburden
Is whiter than wings distinct in a dream.
And Yuletide mirrors reflected
Neither good luck nor a warning.

1986

Надичествовать как орфографическое «твердо»
В несчастный час,
Когда под городом ворочается пустота
И рвутся цепи звонких окон,
Освобождая грани
От крепости углов,
А путник, соболезнуя владельцам штучной рухляди,
Имуществует без потерь.

1987

To be present like an orthographic "aitch"
In an unhappy hour,
When the void tosses and turns under the city
And chains of ringing windows burst,
Liberating the walls
From the from the firmness of angles,
But a wayfarer, sympathizing with the owners of inherited goods,
Takes indifferent possession.

1987

Оставив девочек в декокте мелководья, девой
Явиться из ребра вольны.
Бесследно отмель миновав, на берег
Взойти — разводистые лунки
По ситцу. Грудь и бедра
(У кончика ноги цветущий подорожник.)
Оправить вязкой сетью.
И множиться в зрачках и на устах.

1987

Girls left in a decoction of shallows, a virgin
Emerges from the edge of a wave.
Without leaving a trace in the sand, to climb up
On the berm—discolored openings
In the chintz. Breast and thigh
(A plantain flowering at the stem of her leg,)
Set right in an intractable net.
Burgeoning deep in the eyes and on the lips.

1987

Нет, не грустить о славных временах
Народных пирожков с начинкой
Из ливера эретиков, — но, скажем, примерять личины
(Напялил, сдовно маску, кости таза,
Изящно позвоночник изгонул,
Подобно хоботу противогаза,
И стал неузнаваем вельзевул.) и
Беседовать о самоценности плацебо.

1992

No, not to grieve for the celebrated times
Of folkloric pies stuffed with
The guts of heretics, —but, let's say, to try on disguises
(I put on, like a mask, pelvic bones,
A spinal column gracefully bent
Like the proboscis of a gas-mask,
And became unrecognizable beelzebub.) and
To chat about the placebo of self-worth.

1992

Полночная констелляция,
Пруд — лоно лунно — без морщинки,
И — тени, тени, тени . . . — акустическое одиночество.
Упругую поверхность возмутить
(Затрепетала спугнутая элодея.)
Припав губами. Жажда —
Извечнее
И приснее воды?

1992

Midnight constellation,
A pond—lunar lapping—without a ripple,
And—shadows, shadows, shadows . . . —acoustical solitude.
To agitate an elastic surface
(Exhausted frightened elodea.)
Lips have pressed. Is thirst
more sempiternal
and more everlasting than water?

1992

Владеть устами — навык или дар,
Когда молчание билабиальней речи? Окольцовывать
(Orbicularis oris) или отвергать.
А гений, ставший на крыло
(Лазоревые кроющие перья, маховые —
Пребелые.), не зависает ли,
Быв удостоен невесомым «Ах!» меж алых семядолей,
Их разомкунувшим?

                                              1992

Is it skill or a gift to govern the lips
When silence is more bilabial than speech? To band
(Orbicularis oris) or to turn away.
And genius, on the wing
(Sky-blue covering feathers beating
Blindingly white.) hovering, yes?
With an earned, weightless "Ah!" among scarlet cotyledons
It had dispersed?

1992

Ираиде

И ликовать
И вдруг впадать в отчаянье, пока одушевленно
Кипение
Еще в стога не сложенного луга
И близок профиль спутицы на фоне
Лилово — розовый намет, подложенный
Лазурью, — видной
Зари.

1993

for Iraida

And rejoice,
And suddenly fall into despair while a lively
Boiling
Still roils the unstacked hay of an open meadow
Nearby, my beloved's profile—on a violet
Background, a gathering of pink, lined
With azure—visible
Dawn.

1993

Будь суждено — *in contumacia* —
Тогда и с палубным билетом
На брандере в лонгшезе
Дремать бы или, на худой конец,
Заняться систематизированием антецедентных
Случайностей и совпадений,
Ан нет — ни выволоченного (Кем?)
На брег челна, ни паруса на горизонте.

1995

Be it judged—*in contumacia*—
And then with a deck ticket
On a fireship in a chaise longue
To doze or if worse came to worst
To be busy with the systemization of antecedents
Of accidents and coincidences,
And nothing to be done—neither a boat dragged (by Whom?)
Onto shore, nor a sail on the horizon.

1993

Войти под кров древесных крон (Фитоценоз
На третий день Творения?), как в храм,
Понеже лесом осязаемо движение
И видимо кипрейным гарям
И вейниковым вырубкам,
И не у всякого дыхания,
Но у растений —
Не сказано ли? — пренатальный опыт смерти.

1996

To go in under the forest canopy (Phytocenosis
On the third day of Creation) as into a temple,
For that the movement in the woods is tangible
And visible to the willow cinders
And to the birch clearings,
And not to just any breathing,
But to plant-growth—
Hasn't it been said?—there is a prenatal experience of death.

1996

Просторной стороной равнина
На юг,
На север памятив лесами.
Безмолвствуя певцом
(На вдохе задержав дыхание?),
Русалок наблюдать
На лунном берегу,
На солнечном — обыкновение монад.

                                        1997

A prairie spacious on the southern
Side,
Memorable for its woods to the north.
The silence of a singer
(Breathing held in a breath?)
To watch mermaids
On the lunar shore,
And on the solar one, an everyday monad.

1997

Краснеет и желтеет чернолесье.
(Как некогда на одеяния —
И то сказать, изжита живость,
Но не ветреность —
За багрецом и золотом не постоял поэт.)
Сезон унылой
Зажиточности спорофитов
Встречать под пологом играющей листвы.

1997

The hardwoods turn yellow and red.
(As in the olden days on his attire—
So to speak, its liveliness toned down,
but not its giddiness—
the poet dispensed with crimson and gold.)
To meet the melancholy
Season when sporophytes prosper
Under a canopy of leaves at play.

1997

М. Ереминой

Течение вытачивает рыбу,
Вынашивает птицу ветер,
Земля
(Неповторимы дни Творения,
Поскольку вечны, сиречь закодировано
Во всякой тварной матрице
Несовершенство воспроизводимого.)
Свидетельствует абыолют зерна.

1998

for M. Yeryomina

The current spins the fish,
The wind bears the bird,
The earth
(Not repeating the days of Creation,
Considering them as eternal, to wit
The imperfection of reproducing
Is encoded in every creaturely matrix)
Certifies the Absolute of the seed.

1998

Ираиде

Бывало, продолжался нежный сумрак перголы
Сюжетом тканых выцветших обоев:
Пониже горнего, повыше дольнего
(В пределах заданных координат.),
На мотыльковых крылышках порхающие,
Упитанные купидоны
(Закон Невтона оным не указ.)
Витают.

2001

for Iraida

The tender twilight of a pergola prolonged
Sometimes by the subject of the faded fabric of shoes:
Lower than the hill, higher than the dale
(Co-ordinates within given limits)
On fluttering moth wings
Well fed little Cupids
(Not at the mercy of Newton's law)
Hover.

2001

Что до слепой стены (Окно —
Источник света
С восходом солнца для жильца,
В ночи — для гостя или пилигрима.),
То не исторгнутся и под ударами судьбы
Из незапроектированного
(Ни створок, ни наличников.) проема
Оскольчатые слезы.

2002

What about the blind wall (The window
Is a source of light
At sunrise for the resident,
During the night—for a guest or a palmer.)
What are not exelled under the blows of fate
Through the absolutely unprepared
(neither panels nor casements) doorway
Are splintered tears.

2002

В. Герасимову

Рассказывают, что в развалинах
Дворцов и замков нечто или некто
Не существует, не живет, но есть,
Мол, если нет, то соблаговолите
Дать объяснение тем голосам,
Которыми в урочные часы
Исходят
Фрагменты стен и сводов.

2004

for V. Gerasimov

They recount how in the ruins of palaces
And fortresses something or someone
Does not exist, does not live, but just is,
They say, if this is not so, then
Deign to explain the voices
That at certain hours
Sound within
These fragmented walls and vaults.

2004

Ираиде

Никак опять чарующ ландыш
В букете, бутоньерке, вазе или склянке
Из-под Tincturæ Convallaria
(Период сбора от бутонизации
До экспликации.) и в перелисице,
Где неумолчного ручья, который
Окатывает экзерсисный гравий краснословия,
Невнятна речь.

2004

for Iraida

The lily of the valley in no way again captivating
In a bouquet, boutonnière, vase or bottle
From under *Tincturæ Convallaria*
(A period of collection from budding
to explication.) and in a stand of trees,
Where in the uninterrupted brook
Practice pebbles of eloquence are flooded by
Indistinct speech.

2004

Ираиде

Потрескивал, искрил (Избыток
Селитры или подмесь твёрдых углеводородов
Чрезмерна?)
В уюте сумерек фитиль, как вдруг электросвет,
Который не древней ли, чем костры,
Лучины и лампады (Не во еьме ли довремён
Метали молнии предтечи громовержцев?),
Разоблачил свечу и выявил житейские углы.

2008

for Iraida

It crackled, it sparked (an excess
Of saltpetre or a grand sweep of hard
Hydrocarbons?)
A cozy wick of twilight, like sudden electric light
No more ancient than campfires,
Kindling, and icon-lamps (Did the forerunners
Of metals fulminate not in the darkness of beforetime?)
Uncovered the candle and revealed ordinary corners.

2008

Ираиде

Когда предзимье гасит цвет за цветом,
Смириться с неизбежной убеленностью
Природы? Оболочь ли зябкие растения заботой
И защитить от выцветанья их наряды?
С дорукотворной дерзко потягаться
Поделочною красотою (Кварцевый песок,
Поташ и окислы тяжелых
Металлов.), орешеченной свинцом?

2009

for Iraida

When will early winter extinguish color after color,
Submit to the inescapable grayness
Of nature? Will a shell shelter plants sensitive to cold
And protect against the fading of their attire?
Can the artificial be rivaled with impunity
By natural beauty (Quartz sand,
Potassium and oxides of heavy
Metals) laced with lead?

2009

Mikhail Fyodorovich Yeryomin was born in 1936 in the northern Caucasus but grew up in Leningrad, where he studied in the Philology Department of the Leningrad State University and graduated from the Herzen Institute. He is a playwright and a translator (of T. S. Eliot, Hart Crane, W. B. Yeats, M. Ikbal, Khushkhal-khan Khattak, among others) who saw few of his poems published in his homeland during the Soviet period. Instead, his work—consistently in eight-line stanzas rich with allusive scientific and linguistic byplay —appeared in émigré journals like *Kontinent* and *Ekho*. The first volume of his poems (in Russian) was published in the United States in 1986, and then in 1991 in Moscow. Each book is a cumulative edition to and a selection from his previous work, and each carries the same title: *Stikhotvorenia* (Poems). In English translation, his poems have appeared in *Contrappasso*, *Fjords Review*, *The Hawai'i Review*, *Naked Punch*, *Parthenon West*, *Stand*, *Two Lines*, and in the anthology *In the Grip of Strange Thoughts*. The poet lives in St. Petersburg.

J. Kates is a poet, literary translator, and the president and co-director of Zephyr Press, a nonprofit press that focuses on contemporary works in translation from Russia, Eastern Europe, and Asia. He has been awarded a National Endowment for the Arts Creative Writing Fellowship in Poetry, a Translation Project Fellowship, an Individual Artist Fellowship from the New Hampshire State Council on the Arts, and the Cliff Becker Book Prize in Translation. He has published three chapbooks of his own poems—*Mappemonde* (Oyster River Press), *Metes and Bounds* (Accents Publishing), and *The Old Testament* (Cold Hub Press)—and a full book, *The Briar Patch* (Hobblebush Books). He is the translator of *The Score of the Game* and *An Offshoot of Sense* by Tatiana Shcherbina; *Say Thank You* and *Level with Us* by Mikhail Aizenberg; *When a Poet Sees a Chestnut Tree* and *Secret Wars* by Jean-Pierre Rosnay; *Corinthian Copper* by Regina Derieva; *Live by Fire* by Aleksey Porvin; and Genrikh Sapgir's *Psalms*. He is the translation editor of *Contemporary Russian Poetry* and the editor of *In the Grip of Strange Thoughts: Russian Poetry in a New Era*. A former president of the American Literary Translators Association, he is also the co-translator of four books of Latin American poetry.

The Cliff Becker Book Prize in Translation

> *"Translation is the medium through which American readers gain greater access to the world. By providing us with as direct a connection as possible to the individual voice of the author, translation provides a window into the heart of a culture."*
> —Cliff Becker, May 16, 2005

Cliff Becker (1964–2005) was the National Endowment for the Arts Literature Director from 1999 to 2005. He began his career at the NEA in 1992 as a literature specialist, was named Acting Director in 1997, and in 1999 became the NEA's Director of Literature.

The publication of this book of translation marks the culmination of work he had done in support of his personal passion for ensuring the arts are accessible to a wide audience and not completely subject to vagaries of the marketplace. During his tenure at the NEA, he expanded support for individual translators and led the development of the NEA Literature Translation Initiative. His efforts did not stop at the workplace, however. He carried out his passion in the kitchen as well as the board room. Cliff could often be seen at home relaxing in his favorite, worn-out, blue T-shirt, which read, "Art Saves Me!" He truly lived by this credo. To ensure that others got the chance to have their lives impacted by uncensored art, Cliff had hoped to create a foundation to support the literary arts which would not be subject to political changes or fluctuations in patronage, but would be marked solely for the purpose of supporting artists, and in particular, the creation and distribution of art which might not otherwise be available. While he could not achieve this goal in his short life time, now, seven years after his untimely passing, his vision has become manifest.

In collaboration with White Pine Press and the Cliff Becker Endowment for the Literary Arts, the Creative Writing Program at the University of Missouri, together with his surviving wife and daughter, has launched an annual publication prize in translation in his memory. The Cliff Becker Book Prize in Translation will produce one volume of literary translation in English, annually, beginning in the fall of 2012. It is our hope that with on-going donations to help grow the Becker Endowment for the Literary Arts, important artists will continue to touch, and perhaps save, lives of those whom they reach through the window of translation.